DATE DUE

American Lives

Clara Barton

Elizabeth Raum

Heinemann Library
Chicago, Illinois

© 2004 Heinemann Library
a division of Reed Elsevier Inc.
Chicago, Illinois

Customer Service 888-454-2279

Visit our website at www.heinemannlibrary.com

Designed by Heinemann Library
Photo research by Janet Lankford Moran
Printed in China by WKT Company Limited.

08 07 06 05 04
10 9 8 7 6 5 4 3 2 1

**Library of Congress Cataloging-in-Publication
Data**
Raum, Elizabeth.
 Clara Barton / Elizabeth Raum.
  v. cm. -- (American lives)
Includes bibliographical references and index.
Contents: Hopes and fears -- Little sister -- Brave
little soldier -- Helper -- Teacher -- Patent clerk --
War -- Angel of the battlefield -- Detective --
Speaking out -- International Red Cross --
American Red Cross -- First aid.
 ISBN 1-4034-4993-7 (hc) -- ISBN 1-4034-5704-2
(pbk.)
1. Barton, Clara, 1821-1912--Juvenile literature.
2. American Red
Cross--Biography--Juvenile literature. 3. Nurses--
United States--Biography--Juvenile literature.
[1. Barton, Clara, 1821-1912. 2. American
National Red Cross. 3. Nurses. 4. Women--
Biography.] I. Title. II. American lives
(Heinemann Library (Firm))
HV569.B3R38 2004
361.7'634'092--dc22
                            2003015750

Acknowledgments
The author and publishers are grateful to the
following for permission to reproduce copyright
material: Title page, p. 17 National Archives and
Records Administration; pp. 4, 8, 10, 11, 13, 14,
20, 27 Library of Congress; p. 5 Mary Evans
Picture Library; pp. 6, 29 Michael Dwyer/AP
Wide World Photos; p. 7 PhotoDisc/Getty Images;
p. 9 North Wind Picture Archive; p. 12 Fort Plain
Free Library; pp. 15, 22 Clara Barton National
Historic Site/National Park Service; pp. 16,
25 Bettmann/Corbis; p. 19 General Services
Administration/AP Wide World Photos; p. 21
Corbis; p. 23 David J. & Janice L. Frent
Collection/Corbis; p. 24 Hulton-Deutsch
Collection/Corbis; p. 26 American Red Cross;
p. 28 Stock Montage, Inc.

Cover photograph by Corbis

The author would like to thank her editor,
Angela McHaney Brown, for her support
and encouragement.

The publisher would like to thank Michelle Rimsa
for her comments in the preparation of this book.

Every effort has been made to contact copyright
holders of any material reproduced in this book.
Any omissions will be rectified in subsequent
printings if notice is given to the publisher.

The cover image of Clara Barton was taken in the
1880s. She was in her sixties.

Contents

Some words are shown in bold, **like this.** You can find out what they mean by looking in the glossary.

Hopes and Fears

Few things made young Clarissa Harlowe Barton happier than listening to her father's war stories. His exciting tales made Clara hope that someday she, too, could be a soldier. But Clara lived in a time when women were expected to become wives and mothers, not soldiers. Few jobs were open to women, and even most teachers and nurses were men. It seemed unlikely that Clara's dreams of serving her country in battle would ever come true.

Clara was president of the American National Red Cross from 1882 to 1904.

Even though she liked hearing about exciting battles, little Clara was shy and easily frightened. She worried about snakes and thunder and runaway horses. Even though Clara loved to learn, she was afraid of the other children at school. They teased her because she spoke with a **lisp** that made it hard to understand her. In time, though, Clara Barton overcame her childhood fears and bravely faced danger.

This is what many classrooms looked like around the time Clara was in school.

Little Sister

The home where Clara was born is now a museum.

Clara Barton was born on December 25, 1821. Her brothers and sisters were so much older than her, they acted more like teachers than like playmates. Clara's sister Sally was almost eleven, her brother David was thirteen, Stephen was fifteen, and Dorothy was seventeen. They called Clara "Tot" or "Baby." They taught her reading, spelling, and basic math. Her brother David taught her to ride horses, something she enjoyed her entire life.

Blackboards like this one were often used at schools in Clara's time.

Clara started school when she was only three years old. On her first day of school, the teacher called on Clara to spell the word *dog*. Clara said that she could already spell three-**syllable** words. Clara loved learning. Sometimes, if she had trouble sleeping, she woke her big sister Sally. Together, they looked at the maps in Clara's **atlas.**

Button

Button, a little white dog with big black eyes, was Clara's only playmate when she was small. He followed Clara everywhere and slept on her bed each night.

7

Growing Up

When Clara was eight, her parents sent her to **boarding school.** They thought being away from home would help Clara make friends. But Clara was so unhappy there, she was sent back home. Clara moved with her parents to a nearby farm to help a family with four children whose father had died. Clara was happy to finally have playmates her own age.

This is the home where Clara began living at age nine.

Ice skating on frozen ponds was something many people enjoyed doing during winter.

Clara explored the woods and barns, rode horses, and climbed trees with the other children. The boys convinced Clara to go ice skating even though her father had told her that girls should not skate.

Clara had a wonderful time until she fell and cut her knee. She bravely faced the pain, though, and the doctor called her a good little soldier.

Helper

When Clara was eleven, her brother David was hurt in a bad fall. For nearly two years, Clara stayed home from school to take care of him. She gave him medicine, fed him, and kept him company. Everyone was amazed that Clara could handle such a big job.

When David recovered, Clara returned to school. Her family wondered what Clara would do after she finished school. She was still very shy.

This is a portrait of David Barton from later in life. Caring for her brother helped Clara learn how to take care of sick people.

The Life of Clara Barton

1821	1832	1839	1854	1862	1867
Born on December 25	Nursed brother David	Became a teacher	Began work as a patent clerk	Helped Civil War soldiers on the battlefield	Joined **suffrage** movement

A family friend suggested that Clara would be a good teacher. Clara passed the required test and was given a teaching job. Clara, whom everyone called Miss Barton, was an excellent teacher. Students liked her even though she was very firm.

After six years of teaching, Miss Barton started her own school in her hometown of North Oxford. She taught there for four years.

In the 1800s, schools were often small, single-room buildings.

1869	1873	1881	1904	1912
Traveled to Europe	*Earned Iron Cross*	*Created American Red Cross*	*Started National First Aid Association*	*Died at age 90*

11

Teacher

After ten years of teaching, Barton decided to take time off to continue her own education. In 1851 she attended the Clinton Liberal Institute. Barton loved learning and did well at her studies. She also made many friends. Some were young men who wanted to marry her, but Barton turned them all down. None matched her idea of the perfect husband. Barton moved to New Jersey and found a teaching job.

The Clinton Liberal Institute is in Clinton, New York.

At the time all the schools in New Jersey were **private schools.** Children had to pay to attend. Barton wanted to start a free **public school** so all children could attend without cost. She began one of the first public schools in New Jersey. On the first day only six students showed up. But by the end of the first year, there was a lot more interest in the school. A new, bigger building had to be built, so all 600 children who lived in the town could go there.

The Clara Barton School is in Bordentown, New Jersey.

Patent Clerk

The town hired a man to run Barton's school, and paid him more than three times as much money as they had paid her. Barton was upset, but she continued to teach until a health problem made her lose her voice. She moved to Washington, D.C., hoping the warmer weather there would help her throat. Friends helped her find a job in the U.S. **Patent** Office copying important **documents** by hand.

This is the U.S. Patent Building where Barton worked.

Barton wrote quickly and clearly and earned a good salary. Very few women worked for the government when Barton began her job in 1854. Some people believed that men and women should not work together in the same office. A few of the men who worked with Barton blew smoke in her face and **insulted** her. Barton ignored them. She felt women deserved the same opportunities as men.

Around 1851, Barton had her photo taken. It is the earliest known photograph of her.

Civil War

In 1861, a Civil War began between the Northern and Southern states. Massachusetts men were among the first to sign up to fight. Many had been Barton's students. They had no supplies, so Barton spent her own money for food and gathered combs, pens, and candles to give to them. When she ran out of money to buy supplies, she wrote letters to friends and neighbors and put ads in newspapers asking people to send supplies for the soldiers.

In this 1861 illustration, Barton is shown overseeing nurses in a Washington Red Cross Hospital.

Barton posed for this photograph in the 1860s.

Soon Barton had to rent three **warehouses** to store the supplies, which included medicines and bandages. She decided to take her supplies to the battlefields where they were needed most.

In 1862 she got permission to take her supplies to a battlefield near Culpeper, Virginia. By the time she arrived, the Army doctors were out of bandages. One doctor later told his wife that Barton appeared out of the night like an angel.

Angel of the Battlefield

Barton brought medicine and bandages to the doctors, and food and water to the soldiers. She cooked, helped the doctors, and helped wounded men write letters home. Guns and cannons fired nearby, but Barton refused to leave the battlefield. She did not stop for food or sleep if there was work to do. She helped soldiers from both the North and the South. She helped anyone who needed what she had to give.

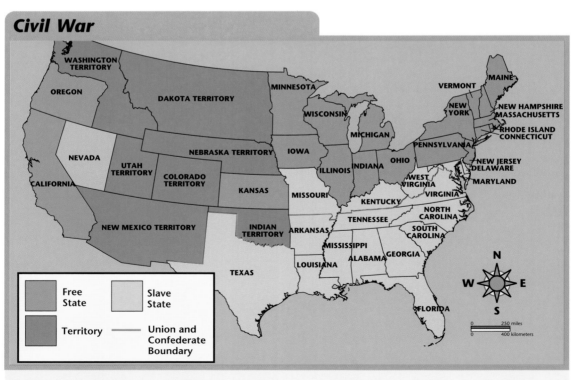

Civil War

The nation was divided over the issue of states' rights.

Barton helped the family and friends of missing soldiers find out what had happened to them.

Barton was happiest when she was helping others. Soon people everywhere heard stories of Clara Barton, the "angel of the battlefield."

When the war ended, people wrote to Barton to ask about their sons or brothers who were missing. Many soldiers had died during the war, but no one had kept track of their names. Others were wounded and unable to write home. Soon Barton had a new job finding missing soldiers.

Detective

President Abraham Lincoln told people that Barton would help them search for missing soldiers. She received thousands of letters. She sorted through them and made a list of the names of missing men. Then she had the list printed in newspapers and displayed in post offices. Anyone who had information was asked to contact Barton. She passed along any news she received. Slowly, she was able to help people find out what had happened to 22,000 soldiers.

There were many lists printed during the Civil War that showed the names of missing soldiers.

ROLL OF MISSING MEN.—NO. 1.

Barton helped to create a national **cemetery** at the Andersonville Confederate prison camp.

Dorence Atwater, who had been a soldier, made a list of men who had died at a prison in Andersonville, Georgia. He gave his list to the government and told Barton about it. Barton got the list, then she and Atwater went to Georgia to visit the former prison camp. She saw the terrible conditions at the prison camp. She knew that many of the men would have survived with medicine, good food, and clean water.

Speaking Out

Barton returned to Washington to learn that her **Patent** Office job had ended. She had spent over $7,500 of her own money to help the soldiers. Now all her money was gone.

Barton wanted to continue searching for missing soldiers, but she needed money to do so. A friend suggested that Barton earn money by speaking about her battlefield work. From 1866 to 1868, Barton spoke to thousands about her war work. At nearly every stop, soldiers thanked her for her help.

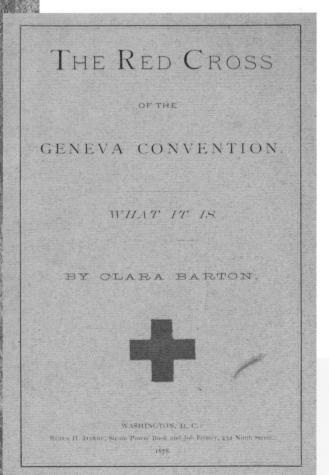

THE RED CROSS

OF THE

GENEVA CONVENTION.

WHAT IT IS

BY CLARA BARTON.

WASHINGTON, D. C.:
RUFUS H. DARBY, Steam Power Book and Job Printer, 432 Ninth Street.
1878.

Barton wrote this to explain her work to others. She hoped people would support her efforts.

Barton joined the many women working for the cause of women's suffrage.

GIVE MOTHER THE VOTE
WE NEED IT

VOTES FOR OUR MOTHERS

OUR FOOD   OUR HEALTH   OUR PLAY
OUR HOMES   OUR SCHOOLS   OUR WORK
ARE   RULED   BY   MEN'S   VOTES

Isn't it a funny thing
That Father cannot see
Why Mother ought to have a vote
On how these things should be?

THINK IT OVER

In 1867, Barton met Susan B. Anthony and Elizabeth Cady Stanton, leaders in the fight for women's **suffrage,** or the right to vote. Barton believed that women should have the same rights as men. In 1867 women could not vote in elections. Barton started to write articles and make speeches in favor of women's suffrage.

International Red Cross

Barton became sick after her speaking tour. She needed to take a break from her busy schedule. Barton and her sister Sally traveled to Europe.

Churches were often used as military hospitals during the Franco-Prussian War.

While there she met a man named Dr. Louis Appia, who told her about a new **organization** called the **International** Red Cross. Members of the Red Cross helped soldiers during wars. They hoped Barton would start a Red Cross organization in the United States.

Clara Barton Firsts

- *First American woman awarded Germany's highest honor, the Iron Cross*
- *First president of the American Red Cross*
- *First woman to represent the U.S. government at an international event*

While Barton was still in Europe, a war began between France and Germany. Barton immediately offered to help the International Red Cross. She spent months working with **refugees** who had lost their homes during the war.

Kaiser Wilhelm, the ruler of Germany, awarded Barton the Iron Cross for bravery and leadership. Barton returned home in 1873 ready to start a Red Cross in the United States.

In this illustration, Barton is shown entering Strasburg with the German Army. The Red Cross flag is shown in the upper left hand corner.

American Red Cross

Barton tried to convince the U.S. government to join the **International** Red Cross. At first, no one seemed interested. But Barton did not give up. She knew that the Red Cross would be a good way to help people during wars, floods, hurricanes, fires, or other **disasters.** Barton did not wait for the government. In 1881 she set up the first **chapter** of the American National Red Cross in Dansville, New York.

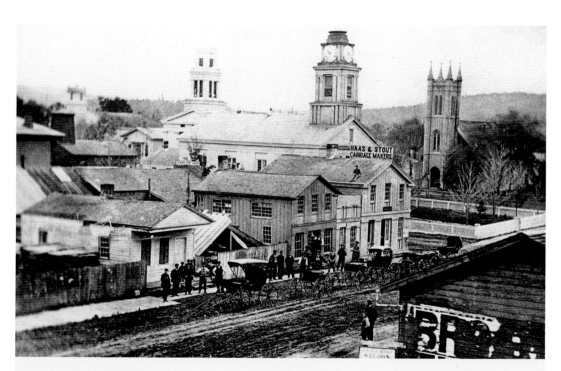

Barton lived in Dansville from 1876 to 1886.

In September of 1881, a forest fire killed 500 people in eastern Michigan. Barton's Red Cross came to the rescue. Newspapers **praised** the Red Cross. Soon Red Cross workers were called to help in other **disasters.** They helped during the Mississippi River floods of 1882 and 1883, an Illinois tornado in 1888, and flooding in Johnstown, Pennsylvania, in 1889.

This was Barton's room at the Beaufort, South Carolina, Red Cross office.

Later Years

Running the Red Cross took most of Barton's time. She also spent about six months in 1883 running a women's prison in Massachusetts.

In 1898, when Barton was 77, she returned to the battlefield for a year to help soldiers fighting in Cuba and to help the Cuban people. When she was 83, she **retired** after 23 years as president of the Red Cross, but she never stopped helping people.

Barton is shown here (seated) with nurses and doctors in Havana, Cuba.

In 1904 Barton started an **organization** called the National First Aid Association. This group taught people how to make first aid kits and to help in **emergencies.**

Clara Barton died in her home in Glen Echo, Maryland, on April 12, 1912. She was 90 years old. The work she began in her lifetime continues today. The American Red Cross still helps people throughout the world during wars or **disasters.**

One of the original first aid kits is now on display at the Clara Barton Museum in North Oxford.

Glossary

atlas book of maps

boarding school school that provides food and housing

cemetery place to bury the dead

chapter group

disaster event that causes great harm

document written record

emergency sudden, unexpected event

insult to hurt someone's feelings

international including many nations

lisp speech problem

organization group with a special purpose

patent legal document that gives an inventor the right to make and sell an invention

praise to admire

private school school that charges students a fee to attend

public school school run by a town, city or state that provides free education

refugee person who flees his country

retire to leave a job or position

suffrage right to vote

syllable part of a word pronounced as a single sound

warehouse building where goods are stored

More Books to Read

Francis, Dorothy Brenner. *Clara Barton*. Brooklyn: Millbrook Press, 2002.

Klingel, Cynthia and Robert B. Noyed. *Clara Barton*. Chanhassen, Minn.: Child's World, 2003.

Mara, Wil. *Clara Barton*. Danbury, Conn.: Children's Press, 2002.

Woodworth, Deborah. *Compassion: The Story of Clara Barton*. Chanhassen, Minn.: Child's World, 1998.

Places to Visit

Clara Barton Birthplace Museum
  Clara Barton Road
  North Oxford, Massachusetts 01537
  Visitor Information: (508) 987-2056

Clara Barton National Historic Site
  5801 Oxford Road
  Glen Echo, Maryland 20812
  Visitor Information: (301) 492-6245

Index